21st
Century
Junior
Library

PLANTS NEED SUNLIGHT

by Christine Petersen

CHERRY LAKE PUBLISHING * ANN ARBOR, MICHIGAN

CHERRY
LAKE
Publishing

Published in the United States of America by Cherry Lake Publishing
Ann Arbor, Michigan
www.cherrylakepublishing.com

Content Adviser: Sharon Castle, PhD, Associate Professor of Elementary Social Studies, George Mason
University, Fairfax, Virginia

Reading Consultant: Cecilia Minden-Cupp, PhD, Literacy Specialist and Author

Photo Credits: Cover and page 4, ©Elena Elisseeva, used under license from Shutterstock, Inc.; cover
and page 6, ©Yusia, used under license from Shutterstock, Inc.; page 8, ©imagebroker/Alamy; page
10, ©Katrina Leigh, used under license from Shutterstock, Inc.; page 12, ©Smit, used under license
from Shutterstock, Inc.; page 14, ©Runk/Schoenberger/Alamy; cover and page 16, ©Sandra Cun-
ningham, used under license from Shutterstock, Inc.; cover and page 18, ©iStockphoto.com/pejft;
page 20, ©Holger Mette, used under license from Shutterstock, Inc.

LIBRARY OF CONGRESS CATALOGING-IN-PUBLICATION DATA
Petersen, Christine.
  Plants need sunlight / by Christine Petersen.
    p. cm. —(21st century junior library)
  Includes bibliographical references and index.
  ISBN-13: 978-1-60279-273-9
  ISBN-10: 1-60279-273-9
  1. Plants—Effect of light on—Juvenile literature. 2. Science—Juvenile
literature. I. Title. II. Series.
  QK757.P43 2008
  572'.42—dc22   2008010473

*Cherry Lake Publishing would like to acknowledge the work of
The Partnership for 21st Century Skills.
Please visit* www.21stcenturyskills.org *for more information.*

CONTENTS

All plants need water to live and grow.

What Do Plants Eat?

Have you ever wondered what plants eat? The truth is amazing. Plants don't eat at all! Instead, plants make food inside their bodies. They need only three main **ingredients**. The first is water. The second is air. The most important ingredient is light. The food that plants make gives them the energy to live and grow.

Roots help plants get nutrients and water.

Plants also need **nutrients** to stay healthy. Nutrients are not food. They are other things found in soil and water that help plants grow. Plants pull them out of soil or water through their roots.

Look!

Find out how light affects plants. Take a photograph of two small plants. Then put one plant in a closet. Put the other plant near a window. Water both plants a little bit every day. After a week, look at the plants again. Compare them to the photograph you took. How has each plant changed?

Some greenhouses have special lamps to help plants grow.

Sunlight is important for plants that grow in the wild. Some plants are raised inside a **greenhouse**. A greenhouse is a building that has the right conditions for growing plants. Greenhouses may use lamps to give plants extra light. Plants can grow under these lamps.

Let's take a closer look at how plants use light.

A plant has few leaves early in its life.

Making Food

Plants usually make food in their leaves. Do you remember the three main ingredients plants need? They are water, air, and light. But how do the ingredients get into the leaves?

Can you see the veins in this leaf?

A plant's roots are like straws. They grow down into the soil. They suck up the water and nutrients hidden there. Water flows up through the stem in **veins**. These are like tiny pipes that lead to every part of the plant. The water spreads to all the leaves.

A thin skin covers the outside of each leaf. You'd be surprised if you saw the skin through a **microscope**. It has thousands of tiny holes. Air flows into the leaf when the holes are open.

This is a picture of a leaf as seen under a microscope. Can you see the tiny green blocks?

A leaf looks green. But the skin is clear, like a window. Light can shine right through it. Inside the leaf are parts that look like tiny green blocks. These parts give the leaf its green color. Their job is to trap light energy.

The leaf uses sunlight energy to put air and water together. It makes a kind of thick liquid sugar. This is the plant's food. Plant food flows out of the leaf to every part of the plant. It flows through the plant's veins.

A sunflower can have hundreds of seeds.

Energy from food helps the plant grow. Food is used to make deeper roots and more leaves. The plant also needs energy to make seeds. If the plant gets enough sun and water, it can make extra food. This is stored in the plant's body. The energy can be used later.

Ask Questions!

Some plants need a lot of sunlight to make food. Others need just a little. Visit a garden center or farm. Talk to people who work there. Ask questions about different kinds of plants. Find out how much sunlight each kind of plant needs.

A squirrel can get food energy from eating apples.

Sunlight in Your Food

Picture yourself eating an apple. What a delicious snack! The apple tree made it using energy from sunlight. You get food energy from the apple. The energy from food helps you play, think, and grow.

Pandas eat bamboo plants.

Food energy passes from plants to animals to other animals. This is called a food chain. Some animals eat plants. Some animals eat other animals. Every animal on Earth is part of a food chain. Almost all food chains begin with sunlight.

Plants need sunlight. You need plants!

Make a Guess!

Think of an animal. Then guess if it eats plants, other animals, or both. Ask an adult to help you find the answer online or in a book. Was your guess correct?

GLOSSARY

greenhouse (GREEN-hous) a building where plants are grown

ingredients (in-GREE-dee-ents) things that are used to make something

microscope (MYE-kruh-skope) a tool that uses lenses to magnify very small things so they can be seen

nutrients (NOO-tree-uhnts) materials found in soil and water that keep plants healthy

veins (VAYNZ) tubes that carry sugar, water, and nutrients through a plant

FIND OUT MORE

BOOKS

Kalman, Bobbie. *Photosynthesis: Changing Sunlight into Food*. New York: Crabtree Publishing Company, 2005.

Star, Fleur. *Plant*. London: DK Publishing Inc., 2005.

WEB SITES

Biology of Plants: Making Food
www.mbgnet.net/bioplants/ food.html
See how plants make food

Glossopedia: Plants
www.globio.org/glossopedia/ article.aspx?art_id=30
Learn more about plants and photosynthesis

INDEX

ABOUT THE AUTHOR

Christine Petersen is a freelance writer and environmental educator who lives in Minnesota. When she is not writing, Christine enjoys kayaking, bird-watching, and playing with her young son. She is the author of more than 20 books for young people.